A Pictorial History of Algonquin Provincial Park

AF207950

1995

First Printed 1977,
Revised and Reprinted 1978, 1980, 1986, 1991, and 1995

By Ron Tozer and Dan Strickland

Fire Ranger Edward Godin on Grand Lake, near Achray, *c.* 1920.
(Ministry of Natural Resources; APM # 1133)

Published by:

The Friends of
Algonquin Park
P.O. Box 248
Whitney, Ontario
K0J 2M0

In Cooperation with:

Ministry of
Natural
Resources
Ontario

Cover Photo: An eastbound train enters Algonquin Park Station, Cache Lake, 1919. In the background can be seen the Park Headquarters buildings (left) and Highland Inn (right). Cache Lake was the main centre of activity along the railway in those early years. None of the buildings remain today. *(National Film Board, Public Archives of Canada – C-84261; APM # 1634)*

Algonquin Provincial Park - A Legacy

There is no doubt that Algonquin Park occupies a very special place in the hearts and minds of Ontario's residents and visitors. Hardly a week goes by that we do not see or hear the name Algonquin in the press or on the radio. Hundreds of letters of enquiry from all over the world arrive in the Park every month. Well over forty books have been inspired in whole or in part by Algonquin, and the list keeps on growing. There is even an Algonquin symphony. And more than 1800 scientific papers have been based on work conducted here, making Algonquin the most important single area in Canada for biological research.

Even more important is the fact that literally millions of people alive today have precious memories of an Algonquin experience — perhaps that unforgettable fishing trip twenty years ago, perhaps falling asleep after a hard day with the wild calls of loons reverberating from ancient, moonlit hills, or perhaps marvelling from a cliff top at wild, rugged country stretching as far as the eye can see.

Indeed, as a refuge from our increasingly strident, urban way of life, Algonquin's nearly 7725 square km of forests, lakes and rivers have assumed an almost incalculable importance as a living link with a vanishing past. How many city children have, or will, come to Algonquin and hear for the first and only time in their lives the mournful howl of a wolf? How many will see first hand — in Algonquin and nowhere else — a reasonable facsimile of the wilderness that once covered all of Ontario?

There is no denying this present and future value of Ontario's oldest, and largest accessible provincial park. But even today, Algonquin's wildness stands in such contrast to the man-created environments we live in that many of us make the mistake of assuming that the Park as we see it now is *exactly* the way it has always been, and that man has had *no* influence on it. This is unfortunate, because in fact, we humans have been associated with the Park area for at least 4500 years, and have been an increasingly major factor in its ecology for the last century and a half. Not only is an understanding of this involvement essential for a realistic appreciation of the present-day Algonquin, but also the various chapters of the Park's history are extremely interesting in and of themselves. It can be said that several important periods of Park history were examples of widespread developments of major significance to the country as a whole. For example, it is a little known fact that at one time over half the able-bodied men in Canada spent their winters in the bush "hurling down the pine" — in the Park area and everywhere else our hard-working, great grandfathers found majestic pines towering above the forest.

This and other eras of Park and Canadian history have long since ended. We will never be able to see for ourselves just what life was like at an Indian campsite, even though successive Indian cultures used the Park area for thousands of years, coming up into our highlands each fall to spend the winter on traditional, family-held hunting territories. Except to the highly trained eye of the archaeologist, about all that remains of this first and longest period of human use is the Park's name. "Algonquin" is a French name that was originally applied to all of more than thirty Indian nations living in northeastern North America and who spoke very similar languages. These included nations we now know as the Ojibwa, Crees, Abenakis, Ottawas, Nipissings, and many others. Today, these linguistically allied people are collectively no longer known as Algonquins but as Algonquians. The old term Algonquin is reserved for just one particular Algonquian nation, the one that was living in the Ottawa Valley at the time of European contact in the early 1600s.

We have much more tangible evidence of subsequent periods of Park history, not only because many physical signs are still in evidence, but also because an astonishing amount of our recent history was recorded on film. Thanks to this fact we can still appreciate today such colourful periods in Algonquin history as those of the pioneer loggers, the early rangers, the hotels, and the railroad.

In this book we present 85 of the best and most representative historical photographs in the Park Archives. We hope you will find them interesting and enjoyable.

References

For further reading about Algonquin Park history, we recommend the following books:

1. *Early Days in Algonquin Park* by Ottelyn Addison, 1985 (First Printed 1974), The Friends of Algonquin Park, Whitney, 144 pp.
2. *Algonquin Story* by Audrey Saunders, 1963 (First Printed 1946), Ontario Department of Lands and Forests, Toronto, 196 pp.
3. *Tom Thomson — The Algonquin Years* by Ottelyn Addison, with Elizabeth Harwood, 1969, Ryerson Press, Toronto, 98 pp.
4. *Tom Thomson: The Silence and the Storm* by Harold Town and David P. Silcox, 1977, McClelland & Stewart, Toronto, 240 pp.
5. *Hurling Down the Pine* by John W. Hughson and Courtney C.J. Bond, 1964, The Historical Society of the Gatineau, Old Chelsea, Quebec, 130 pp.
6. *A Hundred Years A-Fellin'* by Charlotte Whitton, 1974 (First Printed 1943), The Runge Press, Ltd., Ottawa, 172 pp.
7. *Pringrove Through the Years* by Edmund H. Kase, Jr., 1975, (published by the author), 237 pp.
8. *Jack Gervais — Ranger and Friend* by Edmund H. Kase, Jr., 1970, (published by the author), 61 pp.
9. *Camping in the Muskoka Region — A Story about Algonquin Park* by James Dickson, 1959 (First Printed 1886), Ontario Department of Lands and Forests, Toronto, 164 pp.
10. *The Upper Ottawa Valley* by Clyde C. Kennedy, 1970, Renfrew County Council, Pembroke, Ontario, 256 pp.
11. *Great Britain's Woodyard* by Arthur R.M. Lower, 1973, McGill-Queen's University Press, Montreal, 271 pp.
12. *Renewing Nature's Wealth* by Richard S. Lambert, with Paul Pross, 1967, Ontario Department of Lands and Forests, Toronto, 630 pp.
13. *Along the Trail — with Ralph Bice in Algonquin Park* by Ralph Bice, 1980, Consolidated Amethyst Communications, Inc., Toronto, 152 pp.
14. *A Few Rustic Huts* by Sandy R. Gage, 1985, Mosaic Press, Oakville, Ontario, 93 pp.
15. *Early Loggers and the Sawmill* by Peter Adams, 1981, Crabtree Publishing Co., Toronto, 64 pp.
16. *The Lumberjacks* by Donald MacKay, 1978, McGraw-Hill Ryerson, Ltd., Toronto, 319 pp.
17. *A Chronology of Algonquin Provincial Park* by Rory MacKay, 1993 (First Printed 1988), The Friends of Algonquin Park, Whitney, 21 pp.
18. *Glimpses of Algonquin: Thirty Personal Impressions from Earliest Times to the Present* compiled by G.D. Garland, 1994 (First Printed 1989), The Friends of Algonquin Park, Whitney, 163 pp.
19. *The Park and its People: Algonquin* by Liz Lundell and Donald Standfield, 1993, McClelland & Stewart, Inc., Toronto, 196 pp.
20. *Algonquin* by Roderick MacKay and William Reynolds, 1993, Stoddard Publishing Co., Ltd., Toronto, 119 pp.
21. *Names of Algonquin* by G.D. Garland, 1993 (First Printed 1991), The Friends of Algonquin Park, Whitney, 60 pp.
22. *Algonquin Logging Museum: Logging History in Algonquin Provincial Park* by Dan Strickland, 1994 (First Printed 1993), The Friends of Algonquin Park, Whitney, 34 pp.
23. *Protected Places: A History of Ontario's Provincial Parks System* by Gerald Killan, 1993, Dundurn Press Ltd., Toronto, 426 pp.

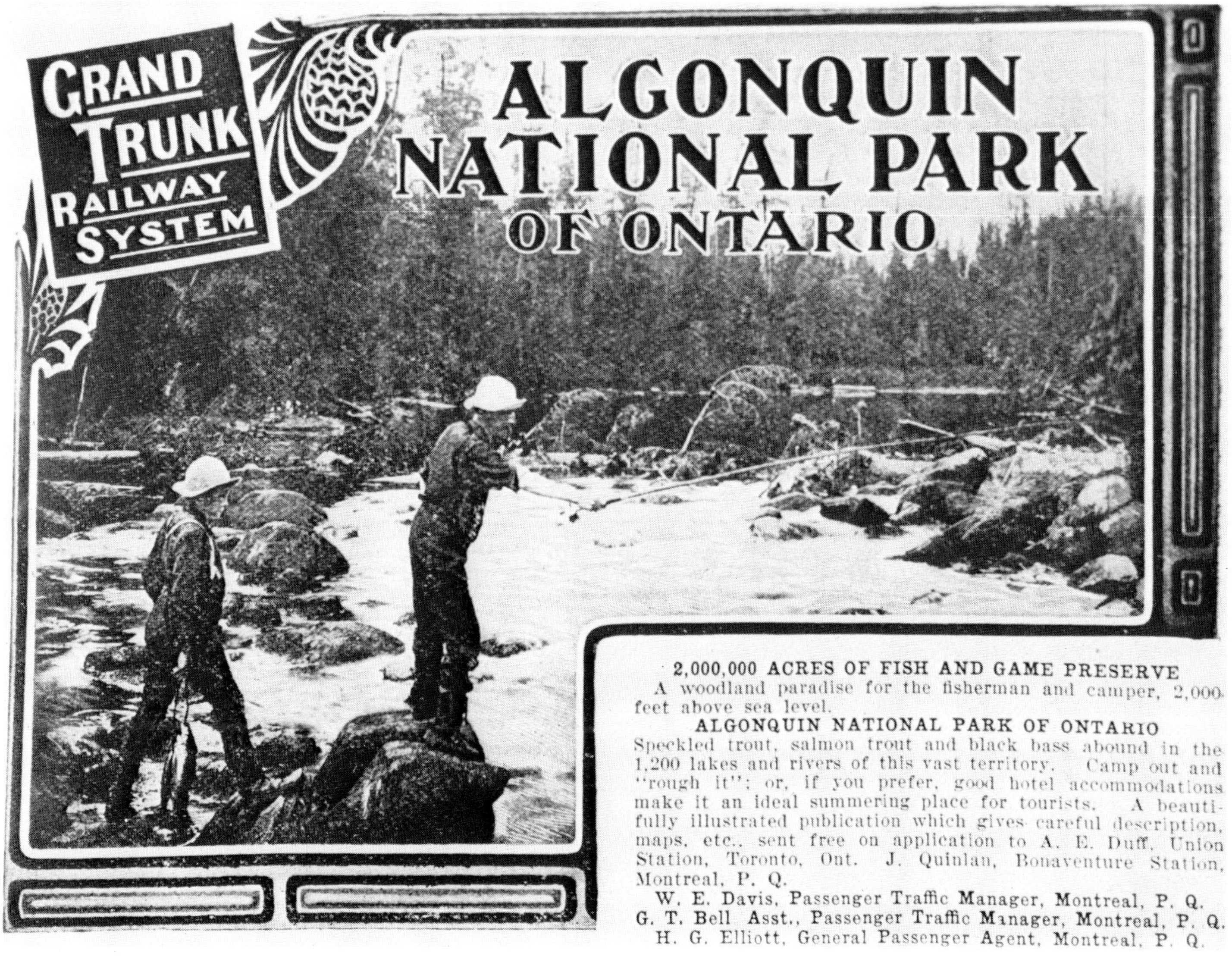

Advertisement for Algonquin "National" Park, appearing in *Rod and Gun* magazine, August, 1911. Although always under the jurisdiction of the Ontario Government, it was not renamed Algonquin Provincial Park until 1913. *(Canadian National Railways; APM #2667)*

A member of the Hayes fishing party with their Indian guides in Algonquin, 1897. George B. Hayes (a prominent industrialist in Buffalo, N.Y.) was one of the earliest regular visitors to the Park area. *(G.B. Hayes; APM #587)*

The Square Timber Era

We do not know who was the first white man to set foot in what is now Algonquin Park. Champlain had come close when he travelled up the Ottawa River in 1615, but he and the missionaries and fur traders who followed him were more interested in pushing west rather than exploring difficult highlands such as the Park area. A few coureurs de bois may have ventured in from time to time, but for the most part Algonquin was unknown to white men until the 1800s. In the early years of that century several British army surveys explored the highlands in search of an alternative water route to the Upper Great Lakes, and to assess the area's potential for agriculture. The Park area was quickly seen to be unsuitable for either purpose, and might very well have gone unvisited again by white men for a long time except for a momentous development in far away Europe.

During the Napoleonic wars at the beginning of the century, the French had cut off the Baltic sources of Britain's ship-building timber. Forced to look elsewhere, England turned to her colonies across the Atlantic, and when Philemon Wright took a small raft of pine down the Ottawa and St. Lawrence rivers to Quebec in 1806, he had no trouble in finding a buyer. This was the start of the square timber trade, and it wasn't long before pioneer loggers were pushing up the Ottawa and its tributaries.

They reached the east side of what is now Algonquin Park in the 1830s, and began the assault on the centuries old Red and White Pines which they found growing there in pure stands. Later they moved on to the scattered White Pine growing among the hardwoods farther west. Only the choicest trees were taken — tall, straight, and free of knots — for anything less would be rejected by the buyers at Quebec. In fact, the buyers demanded that the so-called sticks (up to 20 metres long) be square so that they would fit securely into the holds of ships, saving space and reducing the chance of dangerous load shifts on the storm-tossed Atlantic.

This is why, incredible as it seems today, the pioneer loggers wasted as much as one half of each magnificent tree by squaring them "as smooth as table tops" with their famous broad axes, right in the bush.

The loggers lived an uncompromisingly tough life all winter long in primitive, windowless, "camboose" shanties — each housing 40 to 50 men, two to a bunk. In the early days, their diet consisted only of bread, beans, salt pork, and tea you could "float an axe in". Perhaps once in a winter there would be a visitor — a travelling priest or preacher who ministered to the spiritual needs of these very simple, very tough men, and then passed on to the next camp.

In spring, the timbers were floated down from the Algonquin highlands on the flood waters of swollen lakes and rivers. It sounds easy, but in fact these log drives were even more back-breaking, bone-chilling, and dangerous than work in the winter camps. On the Ottawa River, the square timbers were joined together into huge rafts for the rest of the journey to Quebec. It was often well into the fall before the entire trip was completed, although some longer drives were not finished in one season.

When the square timber era began in the early nineteenth century, it seemed that the supply of big pine was inexhaustible. But just 70 years later it was largely gone. The loggers, and the fires they unwittingly fuelled with the vast amounts of pine slash and chips they left in squaring, had seen to that.

Today, only two small stands of original, big White Pine remain in the Park area — one near the Crow River in the centre of the Park, and the other just outside the southwestern boundary at Dividing Lake.

Giant White Pine — towering 40 m and more into the air, and a metre and a half in diameter — in Algonquin Park, about 1910. The great stands of virgin pine (both Red and White) had brought loggers to the Algonquin highlands by the 1830s. *(Ministry of Natural Resources; APM #968)*

Up to 40 or 50 loggers lived in each camboose shanty, a simple log structure 15 m square with an overlapping scoop roof of logs hollowed out like troughs. The "cambuse" — a raised central fireplace — was vented through a 2 m square hole in the roof. *(Ministry of Natural Resources; APM # 1038)*

The loggers slept in a double tier of bunks (two men in each) around three walls of the shanty. The cook prepared a steady diet of bread and beans (baked in kettles buried in hot sand), salt pork, and strong, green tea in his camboose fireplace. The fire never went out all winter — providing heat and ventilation. *(Public Archives of Canada — C-25718; APM # 1673)*

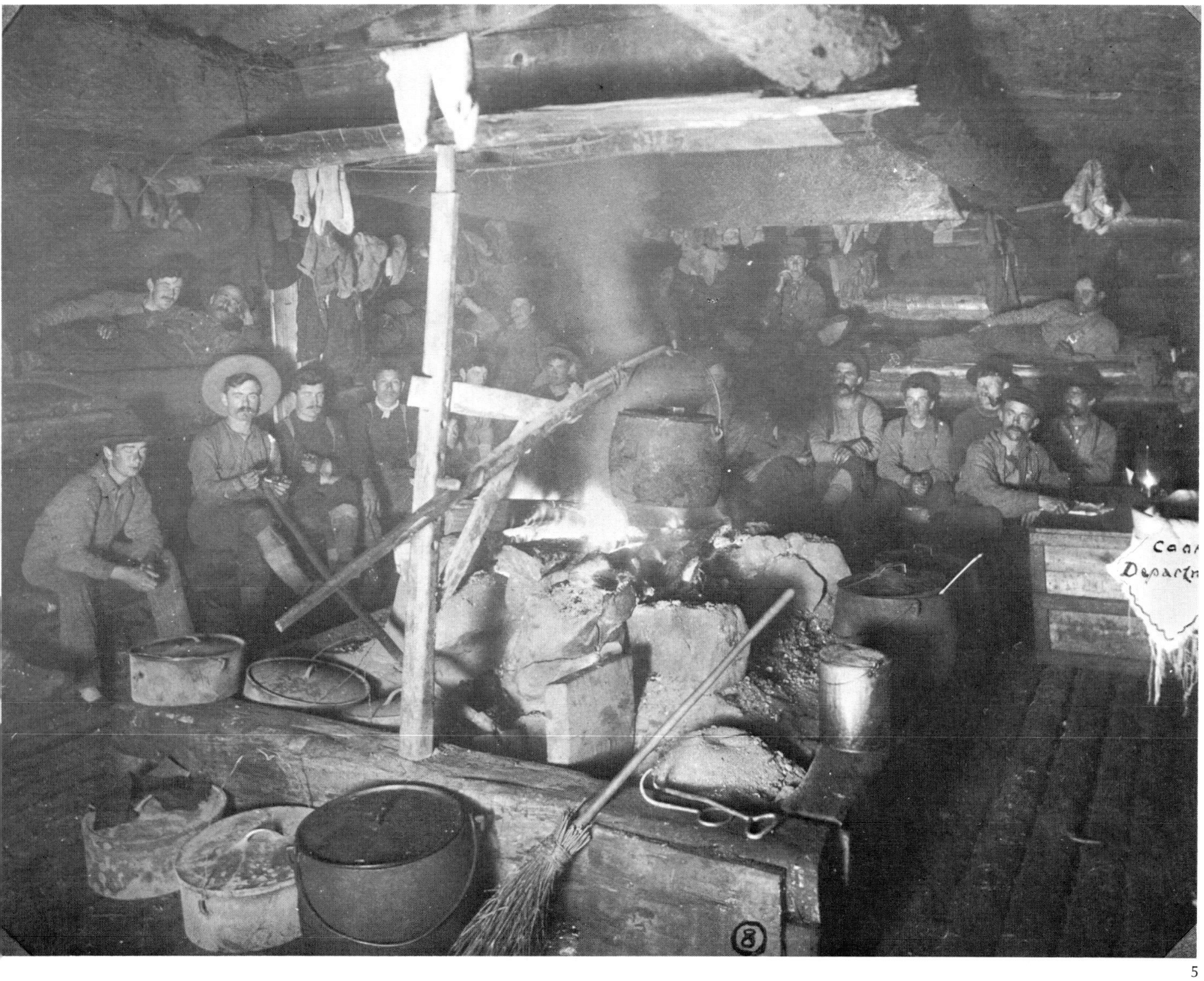

The pine was squared right in the bush, with the older, experienced loggers hewing each side "as smooth as a table top". Squaring lost up to half of the solid wood, but the "sticks" did fit securely in the holds of the timber ships at Quebec. There was no concern for waste, since the supply of pine seemed inexhaustible. *(Ministry of Natural Resources; APM # 1026)*

Each of the completed square timbers was skidded to a clearing, or landing, where they were stockpiled. Later, the logs were hauled by horse-drawn sleigh from the landing to a nearby frozen lake or river. *(Ministry of Natural Resources; APM # 1033)*

The square timbers were dumped on the ice to await spring break-up in late April or early May. Then the log drive would begin, floating the timbers down off the Algonquin highlands on streams, lakes, and rivers to the seaport of Quebec. *(Ministry of Natural Resources; APM # 1247)*

Driving logs in the spring flood was dangerous work which took many lives. No part was more hazardous than breaking up the jams which sometimes formed when the timbers snagged on rocks in the raging torrents. *(Archives of Ontario — L-276; APM # 3276)*

This huge raft of White Pine was cut by the Hale and Booth Co. in Biggar Twp., on the west side of the Park, during the winter of 1889-90. The timbers were driven loose down the Nipissing River to Cedar Lake, and then down the Petawawa and the Ottawa to the mouth of the Bonnechère River, where the raft was constructed for the rest of the journey to Quebec. *(Ministry of Natural Resources; APM # 545)*

Mealtime on a square timber raft. The cook prepared the same simple meals of beans, salt pork, bread, and tea on a sand-filled, raised fireplace under the shelter (right). At the left are the small wooden huts in which the river drivers slept; these shacks were often sold for chicken coops at Quebec! *(Public Archives of Canada — PA-8405; APM # 1124)*

A crib passing through a timber slide at Ottawa. The larger rapids were bypassed by these wooden channels. A raft had to be broken down into individual cribs (each containing about 20 timbers) in order to move through a slide, and then reconstructed again downstream. There might by 100 to 200 cribs in a big raft. *(Public Archives of Canada — PA-8440; APM # 1662)*

Loading square timber into the hold of a timber ship at Sillery Cove, Quebec City. From this seaport, the very best Algonquin pine timbers were shipped to Great Britain. *(Public Archives of Canada — C-4777A: APM # 1659)*

Sawn Lumber Takes Over

Although the square timber trade could not and did not last, its slow decline in no way meant the end of logging in the Algonquin area. For with the increasing scarcity of pine big enough to square, and a decline in the British market, there came a new demand for wood — this time from south of the border. The United States was growing dramatically, pushing westward across treeless prairie; there was a tremendous demand for Canadian wood, not in the form of ponderous square timber, but as sawn lumber. There were still shipments of square timber to Britain after 1850, but increasingly the industry was turning to the production of processed lumber.

This meant the loggers could start taking smaller trees, and dispense with the squaring process. They were floated out as round logs to mills in the Ottawa Valley, established by hard-driving entrepreneurs like the Gillies brothers, MacLachlin brothers, and J.R. Booth, who saw their chance to supply the insatiable American market (and to amass immense personal fortunes).

For the men in the bush, conditions were improving. Iron stoves were introduced to the camps, and depot farms, hacked from the forest, supplied some vegetables to spruce up the devastating monotony of earlier logging camp fare. In the bush, the men now had crosscut saws, and steam-powered amphibious tugs called "alligators" greatly eased the task of hauling log booms across Algonquin lakes.

Still, life was very hard by modern standards. After cutting, the sawlogs were skidded by horse to a landing, where they were stockpiled until teamsters hauled them by horse-drawn sleigh to nearly frozen lakes and rivers. Teenage boys, often fresh off farms in southern Ontario, were frequently employed in cutting skid trails and haul roads. The roads were iced (with water from special tanker sleighs) so that the heavily loaded log sleighs could be pulled by horses. All this had to be done in the dark, long before dawn when hauling would be underway.

The spring log drives of earlier years continued in the sawlog era, but with more and more improvements. Log dams were constructed to control lake levels and their discharge into rivers. (Even today, the levels of many lakes are artificial ones, originally established by these wooden dams.) Where rapids and waterfalls blocked the passage of the logs, long wooden chutes or flumes were built to carry the logs around the obstacles. Even with such improvements, however, log drives remained dangerous — to which many simple graves on the banks of most Algonquin rivers bear silent witness.

The lumber "barons" of this period have assumed almost legendary proportions in the Park area — and perhaps none more so than John Rudolphus Booth. Wherever men gather to recall proudly the stirring tales of the early loggers, J.R.'s name is the first to be mentioned. It was men like him, with a financial interest in the maintenance of forested lands in the Algonquin highlands, who ultimately supported the concept of a "forest reservation and park".

Prime White Pine sawlogs. With the growing American demand for sawn lumber, and an increased number of sawmills in the Ottawa Valley, there was a gradual changeover from square timber production to the cutting of sawlogs in the Algonquin highlands. *(Ministry of Natural Resources; APM # 1057)*

Ⱶ Old Barnet Lumber Co. depot farm on Burntroot Lake, 1959. A depot farm served as a source of supplies for several operating lumber camps on a company's timber limits. Crops such as hay, beans, and potatoes were grown on some of these farms. *(Ministry of Natural Resources; APM # 576)*

Ɣ Main depot camp of the Gilmour Lumber Co. at South Tea Lake, 1893. The lumber shanties were little changed in the early sawlog era, although the scoop roof was often replaced by boards, and the iron stove took over from the camboose fireplace. *(Ministry of Natural Resources; APM # 1093)*

The Munn Lumber Co. cookhouse at Whitefish Lake, 1909. The cooking and eating conditions were becoming less primitive with the addition of stoves and cookhouses. The loggers' basic fare was enhanced with such items as pies, cakes, apples, rice, and jam. *(R. J. Taylor; APM # 3218)*

Water tankers were used to make ice on haul roads to reduce friction on the runners of the heavily loaded logging sleighs. However, hot sand had to be spread on downhill runs to keep the sleighs from overtaking the horses. *(Ministry of Natural Resources; APM # 1091)*

Hauling sawlogs at a landing near Birch Lake, Livingston Twp., 1907. Despite the often bitterly cold temperatures, only the teamsters wore heavy coats. The active work of the other men apparently kept them warm! *(J. W. McNeice; APM # 297)*

Logging dam at Cedar Lake, constructed prior to 1853 and in continuous use until the summer of 1945 when Gillies Brothers Ltd., of Braeside, took their last drive through it. The dam controlled the flow of spring flood waters for floating timbers on the drive. *(R. Thomas and J. Wilkinson; APM # 43)*

A newly constructed timber chute for
Mickle and Dyment Co., between
Ragged and Smoke lakes, 1896. The
chute was built under the direction of
J. W. McNeice in 18 days, using one
team of horses. The rotting remains of
a later chute are still visible today at
this site, although the surrounding
land is now heavily forested.
(J. W. McNeice; APM # 288)

Log chute around rapids on the
Petawawa River, between Catfish
and Cedar lakes. Individual logs
were floated down these flumes on
the flood waters during the drive.
*(R. Thomas and J. Wilkinson;
APM # 19)*

Drivers wading in the cold waters of Aumond Creek during early May, 1902. In order to avoid a jam, they had to keep the sawlogs moving downstream on the spring flood. Soon after breakup there were often chunks of ice floating along with the logs!
(Charles Macnamara Collection, Archives of Ontario — S-5061; APM # 1584)

Log drive on the Petawawa River, 1930. Each log bore the unique stamp of the owner company so that the sea of logs could be sorted and floated to the various company mills on the Ottawa River.
(Canadian National Railway; APM # 1146)

Steam-warping tugs called "alligators" (due to their amphibious capability of winching themselves from lake to lake) were developed to tow booms of logs on lakes. Here, the Barnet Lumber Co. alligator is seen with its log boom and pointer boats on Burntroot Lake, 1908. *(Faculty of Forestry Collection, University of Toronto Archives; APM # 3005)*

J. R. Booth's sawmills, Ottawa, 1907. One of the largest timber operators on the Algonquin highlands, Booth went on to develop what was reportedly the largest company in the world operated by one man. As early as 1870, Booth employed 4000 men in the bush and 2000 men in his mills. *(Public Archives of Canada — PA-8962; APM # 1697)*

The Park's Creation

Algonquin Park was established in 1893, largely thanks to two growing concerns shared by the public and senior civil servants of Ontario. The first person to propose a 20 to 30 township reserve in the area now occupied by the Park was Robert W. Phipps, clerk of forestry in the Ontario Government's Department of Agriculture and Arts. Strongly influenced by growing concerns in North America's agricultural and forestry intelligentsia that the continent's wood supply and climate were being endangered by the rapid, wholesale clearing of forests, Phipps insisted that it was crucial to stop agricultural settlement and land clearing in this part of Ontario. "When covered with extensive woods", he wrote, "the principal heights of land form reservoirs which supply the sources of numerous rivers, give moisture to the numerous small lakes and watercourses … below them, and preserve throughout the whole country a fertility, invariably much impaired when the forests are removed."

Phipps found another strong ally in Alexander Kirkwood, a chief clerk in the Ontario Department of Crown Lands. Once an enthusiastic proponent of agricultural settlement in northern Ontario, Kirkwood had come to realize that most such efforts were doomed to miserable failure and that the land was far better left in forest. He echoed Phipps' ideas on watershed protection and he did his best to marshall as many other practical arguments as he could, putting each one in the most utilitarian light possible. Logging, for example, would continue, controlled so as to achieve "utility and profit". Fur-bearing animals would be protected, partly to preserve them, but also with a view to "taming and domesticating them", again "for use and profit". Even "seekers for health and pleasure" would be accommodated in cottage leases or hotels "offered to public competition at an annual rental". Kirkwood played a key role in swaying opinion and it was he who proposed the name "Algonkin Forest and Park".

For all his advocacy of the Park idea, Kirkwood had never actually set foot in Algonquin and it fell to another man to speak from first-hand experience. James Dickson had surveyed much of the Park area in the 1880s, and had even written a charming book extolling its virtues for outdoor recreation and comparing it favourably with other more famous and faraway beauty spots such as the Rockies. Dickson too, heartily endorsed the idea of an Algonquin Park, but even his testimony wasn't enough to swing the political balance.

The final, decisive push came from a fourth man, Dr. G.A. MacCallum, chairman of a Royal Commission on Game and Fish that the provincial government had been forced to set up by anglers and hunters convinced that Ontario's fish and wildlife were in imminent danger of being destroyed and eliminated. In 1892, MacCallum's final report unequivocally blasted Ontario's existing fish and wildlife management and "strongly and unanimously" recommended the "formation of a provincial game park" as the "best means of restocking the province" with wildlife.

One week later an embarrassed Ontario Government set up another royal commission, with Kirkwood as its chairman, to expedite the creation of the Park, whose existence was now deemed a political imperative. The Commission met only twice and the new Algonquin Park came into being on May 27, 1893.

The original name was "Algonquin National Park", but in fact, the Park has always been under Ontario's jurisdiction. The name was changed to Algonquin Provincial Park in 1913.

Since its creation, Algonquin has been more than doubled in size, to its present 7725 square km, by a series of additions mostly to the east and south of the original Park.

And just as the Park has changed and grown since its original creation, so too have the attitudes and philosophy concerning Algonquin. It comes as a distinct surprise to many people that the Park was not "virgin wilderness", but had in fact been significantly altered by 60 years of logging and man-caused forest fires. Even more surprising is the fact that logging companies welcomed the Park's establishment since it would preserve the valuable forest land from clearing and the increased incidence of fire, which would inevitably result from settlement. In fact, one logging company actually requested the Government to include its limits within the new Algonquin Park.

Alexander Kirkwood — Chief Clerk in the Land Sales Division, Ontario Department of Crown Lands, and supporter of Robert W. Phipps' idea of a "National Forest and Park" in the Algonquin highlands. *(Ministry of Natural Resources; APM # 586)*

James Dickson — Ontario Land Surveyor, who first conducted surveys in the area of the proposed park in 1879, and recommended it for preservation. *(Ministry of Natural Resources; APM # 1474)*

A settler's hut on the Opeongo Colonization Road, an access route for settlement in the Algonquin region. The threat to valuable timber from the clearings and fires created by settlers was an important concern in the Park's establishment. *(Charles Macnamara Collection, Archives of Ontario — S-5056; APM # 1553)*

Burned and cut-over land at Opeongo Forks, 1894. Much of the Algonquin highlands was not a virgin wilderness even at the time of the Park's creation. Logging and man-caused fires had been transforming the area for over 60 years. *(J. W. Ross; APM # 124)*

The Coming of the Railway

The complete compatibility between the Park concept and timber interests in the collective public consciousness of the 1890s is nowhere better illustrated than in the unopposed construction of a railroad across Algonquin just after the Park was created. The Ottawa, Arnprior and Parry Sound Railway was the brainchild of Algonquin's greatest timber baron — J. R. Booth — who conceived of it as a major link in his logging and transportation empire.

Construction of the railway (1894 to 1896) through the rugged terrain of the Canadian Shield was a major engineering feat. Narrow cuts were blasted through the massive Precambrian rock, using dynamite. Then the huge rock fragments were removed by block-and-tackle and horse-drawn sleds. The many low sections and watercourses on the line had to be either filled in with earth and rock, or spanned by massive wooden trestles.

The Mowat townsite (named for the then Premier of Ontario), at the north end of Canoe Lake, became a thriving lumber community of more than 600 people after the coming of the railway. The Gilmour Lumber Co. had a mill there to process the timber from their limits on Algonquin Park's west side, before the operation finally went bankrupt in 1900. The seeds of destruction had been sown with the company's earlier bizarre scheme to float Algonquin timber over a height of land to their mill at Trenton. Ultimately, this project failed due to the time and expense involved, and the inferior quality of the pine. Apart from a few outlines of foundations, a small graveyard, and traces of the railway sidings, there is little at the Mowat site today to remind us of its active past.

In its heyday during World War I, the railroad carried lumber, troops, and western grain. It is even said that at times there was a train every twenty minutes, making the railroad through the Algonquin "wilderness" the busiest in Canada.

The completion of the railway also had a great effect on the recreational use of the new Park, for now the area was truly accessible for the first time. Lodges, youth camps, and leaseholds were reached solely by train for the next 40 years of the Park's existence.

J. R. Booth (in his 98th year) inspecting a special order of waney pine timber salvaged from a burn in the Shirley Lake area, 1924. Booth completed his Ottawa, Arnprior and Parry Sound Railway, through the southern portion of Algonquin Park in 1896. (L. Newman, APM # 384)

In the railway's construction, narrow rock cuts through the rock terrain were blasted out with dynamite. The broken rock was then removed by simple winches and horse-drawn sleds. *(J. W. Ross; APM # 123)*

Many low and swampy sections of the railway required massive filling. Simple horse-drawn scrapers (seen here) and wagons were utilized in this earth-moving work. Several construction companies were contracted to complete different sections of the line. *(J. W. Ross; APM # 135)*

The Islet Lake trestle groans and shakes under the weight of an old wood burning locomotive, in 1896. There were several of these massive wooden bridges on the O.A.P.S. line — a tribute to the skilled workmen who constructed them. *(J. W. Ross; APM # 143)*

Part of the ten acre chip yard of the Gilmour Lumber Co. mill at the Mowat townsite, north end of Canoe Lake. Gilmours shipped pine lumber from this mill by rail, after abandoning the scheme to float Park timber over the height of land to their mill at Trenton. *(R. Thomas and J. Wilkinson; APM # 72)*

Loading logs on a railway flatcar by steam hoist, Lake Opeongo, 1910. This spur line from Whitney to Sproule Bay was built by the St. Anthony Lumber Co. in 1902 to transport timber to their mill. Part of the Opeongo Road follows the old railbed today. *(R. J. Taylor; APM # 3298)*

An eastbound Grand Trunk Railway passenger train stops at Canoe Lake Station, summer, 1916. The coming of the railway led to increased recreational use of Algonquin as the Park became accessible for the first time. *(R. Thomas and J. Wilkinson; APM # 115)*

Early Park Management

Algonquin's first superintendent, Peter Thomson, arrived in the new Park during the summer of 1893, with several of his rangers. They travelled up the Oxtongue River to Canoe Lake, where a site was selected for the Park Headquarters. Thomson soon set out to explore the Park, and establish the first of a series of shelter huts which would accommodate the rangers on their patrols.

By 1900, headquarters had been moved to Cache Lake, and Superintendent George Bartlett had begun his long (1898 to 1922) and eventful tenure in Algonquin. Bartlett took an interest in the introduction of exotic wildlife in Algonquin, (even including European grouse and pheasants) but, except for Smallmouth Bass, none of them was successful. He also experimented with several schemes for raising Park revenues, such as the trapping of furbearers by Park rangers, and the production of maple syrup. Under Bartlett, the ranger staff and system of ranger cabins were expanded to deal with the growing problem of illegal trapping of furbearers in the Park. Since local people had traditionally trapped in the area before its establishment as a Park, many continued to do so after trapping was prohibited. The problem was complicated further when trapping by rangers as a Park revenue source was undertaken between 1908 and 1920. Inevitably, some members of the Park staff became involved in illegal trapping activities for private gain.

The Park's resources were drawn upon when shortages occurred in Ontario's cities during World War I. These efforts included the cutting of firewood, the harvesting of Park deer, and a commercial fishing operation for Whitefish and Lake Trout in Lake Opeongo.

Fire continued to be a major problem against which the Park's fire rangers could do very little until the construction of steel and wooden fire towers in the 1920s and, even more important, the introduction of Park patrol aircraft. In fact, during the tenure of Frank MacDougall, Algonquin's first "Flying Superintendent" (1931 to 1941), the tide was turned in the long struggles against fire in the summer and poachers in the winter.

MacDougall also accurately foresaw that human pressures on Algonquin were going to grow tremendously, and he successfully encouraged the establishment of Park research activities which continue to this day at such facilities as the Harkness Laboratory of Fisheries Research, the Wildlife Research Station, and the Swan Lake Forest Research Station.

George B. Hayes (left), Park visitor from Buffalo, N.Y., meets rangers Tim O'Leary and Steve Waters on patrol, 1897. The loonskins are being stretched for use as moccasin liners in winter. *(G. B. Hayes; APM # 462)*

Ranger shelter hut at Rain Lake, 1897. These cabins (usually of log construction) were built at convenient day's travel distances along the ranger patrol routes. (G. B. Hayes; APM # 61)

Park rangers Albert Ranger (left), Mark Robinson, and Budd Callighen on winter patrol with their dog team. Rangers faced such rigors as breaking trail by snowshoe ahead of their dogs, night temperatures of 40 below, and crossing lakes covered with thin ice or slush. (M. Clare; APM # 2906)

▲ Algonquin Park Headquarters staffhouse under construction at Cache Lake in December, 1896, after the original site on Canoe Lake had been abandoned. We have no information on the two young moose.
(Public Archives of Canada — C-22458; APM # 3876)

▼ George Bartlett (standing), with his family at the Superintendent's house, Cache Lake, 1913. Bartlett (a J. R. Booth Lumber Co. scaler at the time of his appointment) served as Algonquin's superintendent from 1898 to 1922.
(Public Archives of Canada — PA-10701; APM # 1727)

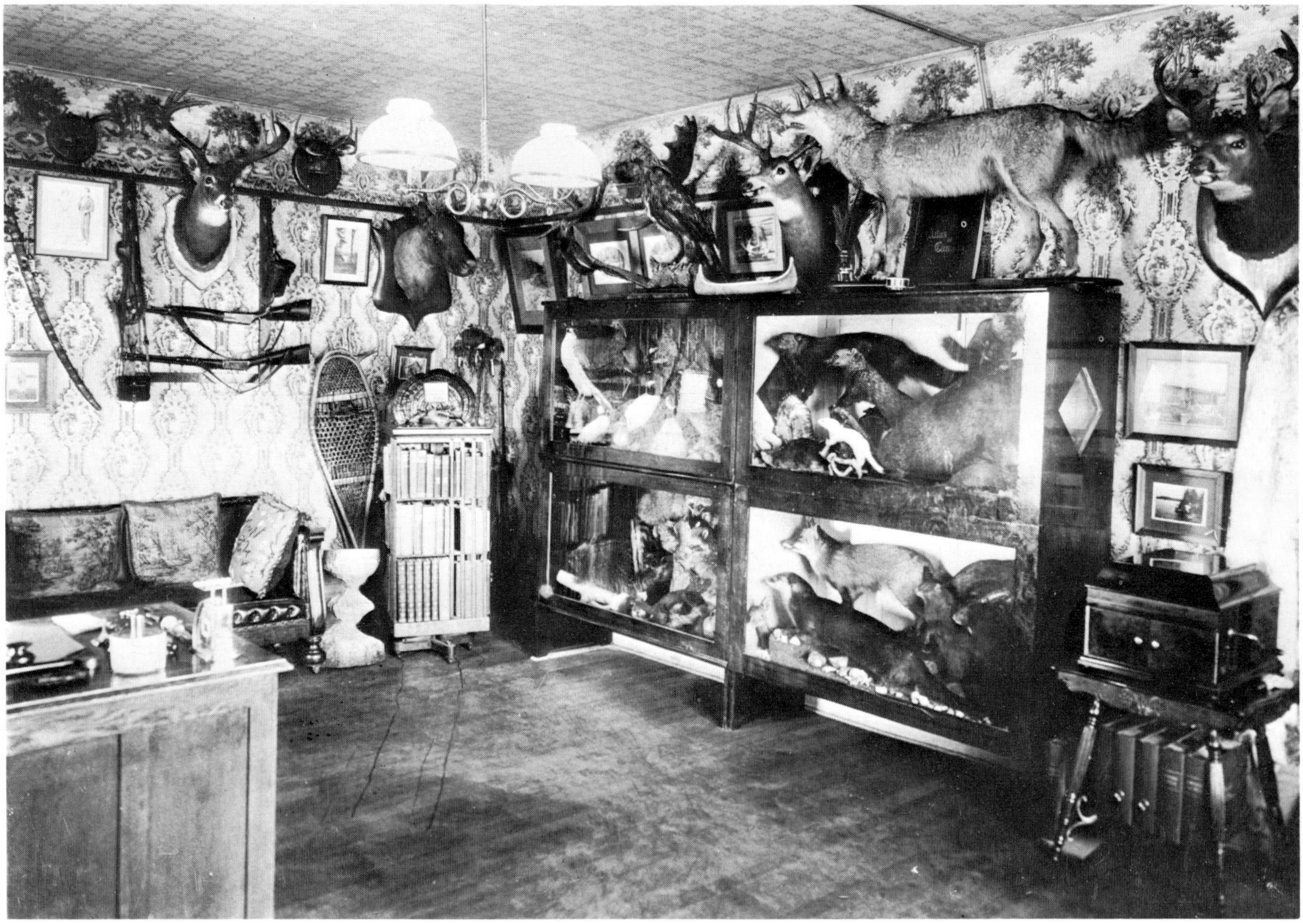

Superintendent George Bartlett's office, Park Headquarters, Cache Lake. Bartlett was keenly interested in the Park's wildlife, and expanded the ranger staff and shelter house system to deal with "pot hunters and poachers". *(O. Addison; APM # 2992)*

Rangers Jim Sawyer (left) and Steve Waters stretching beaver pelts. In order to increase Park revenues, controlled trapping of furbearers by Park staff was introduced by Superintendent Bartlett in 1908. *(S. Waters; APM # 203)*

Traps, snowshoes, and guns at Cache Lake, 1931, confiscated from Algonquin poachers. Illegal trapping by both poachers and some rangers continued to be a major problem until 1932, when winter air patrols began. *(W. N. Bender; APM # 275)*

Ranger Bob Balfour with beaver in a live-trap. In order to publicize the Park, Superintendent Bartlett had beavers live-trapped and sent to zoos all over the world, from 1908 to 1918. *(O. Addison; APM # 2984)*

Park Ranger Bob Balfour (right) with a wolf killed in Algonquin Park, 1916. In the mistaken belief that fewer wolves meant more deer, rangers poisoned (until the 1920s), snared, and shot as many wolves as they could. These attempts at control ended in 1958, when a wolf research program began. *(R. Thomas and J. Wilkinson; APM # 69)*

A load of deer awaiting shipment south by rail, at Algonquin Park Station. In order to alleviate the meat shortage in Ontario during World War I, more than five hundred deer were harvested in the Park during the fall of 1917. *(Ministry of Natural Resources; APM # 1154)*

Another of the projects undertaken by the Park staff to increase revenues was this maple syrup operation on the Minnesing Road, about three miles from Park Headquarters. Although it provided some favourable publicity for Algonquin, profits were small, and so maple syrup production was abandoned in 1942. *(W. N. Bender; APM # 479)*

Wooden fire observation platform built in a White Pine at Smoke Lake by rangers Aubrey Dunne and Max Hubert, 1925. (The tree fell in 1975.) Several steel and wooden fire towers were erected in Algonquin during the early twenties in an effort to combat forest fires. *(R. Carswell; APM # 87)*

Forest fire detection by aircraft began over Algonquin Park as early as 1922, using planes such as the Avro 504K (a First World War night fighter). This one landed that year at the J. R. Booth Lumber Co. Depot at Kiosk. *(R. Thomas and J. Wilkinson; APM # 45)*

Frank MacDougall (right), Algonquin's "Flying Superintendent" from 1931 to 1941, introduced daily Park inspection flights, and expanded forest fire detection operations by air. This picture was taken at Lake of Two Rivers in 1948. *(Ministry of Natural Resources; APM # 3435)*

Activities of fire rangers, such as Joseph Odjack seen here with his family on the Nipissing River, July 1930, included maintenance of the bush telephone lines linking ranger cabins, and cutting of portages. (*Dr. D. A. MacLulich; APM # 2919*)

Ontario Fisheries Research Laboratory staff and truck at their Costello Lake camp (now the picnic ground), 1937. Extensive research on the Park's fish, wildlife, and forests has been undertaken ever since. (*Ministry of Natural Resources; APM # 1962*)

The Lodge Era

The coming of the Ottawa, Arnprior and Parry Sound Railway in 1896 did much more than make money for J.R. Booth. A few adventurers had travelled in the Park before then, but it was the railroad that really made the area accessible to numbers of visitors for the first time.

Several lodges were opened along the line to serve these new visitors, including: Hotel Algonquin on Joe Lake in 1908, Highland Inn on Cache Lake in 1908, Nominigan Camp on Smoke Lake in 1912, Camp Minnesing on Burnt Island Lake in 1913, and Mowat Lodge on Canoe Lake in 1913. These facilities boasted indoor washrooms, hot and cold running water, fine meals, and complete guide and outfitting services. A sometime guide at Mowat Lodge was Tom Thomson, whose brilliant Algonquin sketches and canvases would later place him among Canada's most famous landscape artists.

The Grand Trunk Railway established Nominigan and Minnesing as "wilderness lodges", at bone-jarring distances of eleven and sixteen km by stage from Algonquin Park Station on Cache Lake — for those who wished more primitive conditions. However, even at these "remote wilderness outposts", the guests dressed impeccably by today's standards, and gathered for formal dining in the main lodge. It was a far cry from "roughing it in the bush"!

After completion of the Canadian Northern Railway in 1915, through the northern portion of Algonquin Park, that area became accessible to Park visitors as well. Several lodges were later opened along the line, including Wigwam Lodge at Kiosk, Lake Travers Lodge, and Kish-Kaduk Lodge on Cedar Lake.

Youth camps were established early in Algonquin Park. The first of these was apparently a camp for boys which operated for two or three years on Cache Lake, prior to 1908. Camp Northway Lodge, a girls' camp started by Miss Fannie L. Case in 1906, was established on Cache Lake (near the site of the original boys' camp) in 1908. Several others followed, with the Taylor Statten Camps on Canoe Lake being among the best known — Ahmek for boys established in 1921, and Wapomeo for girls starting in 1924. The Algonquin youth camps have instilled an important feeling for wilderness and a capacity for basic outdoor skills in several generations of young people.

The first private leases on lakeshore lots in Algonquin Park were issued by the Ontario Government early in this century. Ultimately, more than 600 leases were granted before the practice was discontinued in 1954. The 310 currently active leases will expire in 2017.

Eastbound train passes Park Headquarters as it pulls in to Algonquin Park Station, Cache Lake. Several lodges were built along the railway to accommodate the expanding Park tourist trade. *(Public Archives of Canada — PA-20593; APM # 1726)*

The first section of Highland Inn at Cache Lake was opened in 1908 by the Grand Trunk Railway. It had only ten bedrooms, so overflow guests were accommodated in adjacent tents on wooden platforms. (Notice the cow.) *(M. Clare; APM # 2852)*

Highland Inn had three sections when completed in 1910, and could accommodate 150 people. Its facilities included a billiard room, dance pavilion, tennis courts, and bowling green. The hotel was operated by the Canadian National Railway until 1928, and then by private interests, both summer and winter. It was demolished during the mid-fifties. *(Canadian National Railway; APM # 1151)*

▲ Ladies on the verandah of Highland Inn, overlooking Cache Lake, about 1910. The men often went fishing while the women stayed behind at the hotel to chat and play cards. *(M. Clare; APM # 2853)*

▼ A horse-drawn "democrat-taxi" left Highland Inn to carry guests over rough roads to the two "wilderness lodges" established by the Grand Trunk Railway — Nominigan on Smoke Lake, and Minnesing on Burnt Island Lake. *(W. N. Bender; APM # 261)*

▲ Camp Minnesing, built in 1913 on Burnt Island Lake. A C.N.R. brochure described it as "an ideal vacation place in the heart of an immense wilderness.... The dining room service is of the highest order and the meals are all that can be desired. Shipments of fresh fruit, vegetables, and meats are received daily and milk is secured from our own cows." *(M. Pigeon; APM # 2765)*

▽ Guests arriving by launch at Nominigan Camp, Smoke Lake, which opened in 1912. The C.N.R. advertised it as "a log cabin camp similar to those of Maine, of world-wide fame". The row of guest cabins burned down in 1928, but the main lodge stood until 1977. *(Public Archives of Canada — PA-10633; APM # 1733)*

Dining room in the main lodge at Nominigan Camp on Smoke Lake. In 1923, the rates were $30 per week for a single room, with detached bath — including meals! *(M. S. Cooper; APM # 2554)*

The original Mowat Lodge on Canoe Lake, 1917. This building had been a boarding house for the Gilmour Lumber Co. mill. It burned to the ground in November, 1920. A new Mowat Lodge was opened nearby in 1921, but it ultimately suffered the same fate — burning in May, 1930. *(D. Crombie; APM # 2500)*

▲ Tom Thomson — Canada's famous natural landscape artist — frequently stayed at Mowat Lodge while painting his dramatic Algonquin scenes from 1912 until his tragic death in Canoe Lake during July, 1917. Thomson captured the true spirit of Algonquin with paintings such as *The West Wind*, *The Jack Pine*, and *Northern River*. *(Tom Thomson Memorial Gallery; APM # 188)*

▼ Summer Station Agent at Joe Lake Station about 1921. The only log station on the line, Joe Lake was the terminus for guests staying at the nearby Hotel Algonquin (built in 1908). *(I. Hambleton; APM # 2147)*

Hotel Algonquin was a rustic structure situated back from the railway station on a hill over-looking Joe Lake. Edwin Colson, who bought the hotel in 1917, also operated a well-equipped outfitting store nearby. All these buildings were demolished during the 1950s, under a policy of returning the Park to a more natural state. *(Ministry of Natural Resources; APM # 620)*

A group of girls in their camp uniforms start out on a canoe trip from Northway Lodge (a youth camp on Cache Lake) in 1915. Several camps for girls and boys were established in Algonquin during these early year. *(W. A. Mudge; APM # 1306)*

An increasing number of canoeists were exploring the Algonquin "wilderness" during this era, also. This camp on Crown Lake belonged to a party that travelled through Smoke and Ragged lakes about 1912. *(Public Archives of Canada — C-56127; APM # 1736))*

The Ontario Government actively sought to increase Park use during these early years by offering long term leases on lakeshore cottage lots. This Canadian National Exhibition display in Toronto during 1932 advertised the availability of leaseholds in Algonquin. The policy of leasing new land was discontinued in 1954. *(W. N. Bender; APM # 430)*

The "Hotel Crowd" waiting for the train at Algonquin Park Station, Cache Lake, 1929. The railway was *the* means of transportation for the many people coming to Algonquin's lodges, camps, and leaseholds until 1935. *(H. M. King; APM # 1170)*

Algonquin Park Station, Cache Lake, in the 1940s. The railway and lodges rapidly declined after Highway 60 was built in the thirties, and car camping boomed after World War II. The last train came to Cache Lake in 1959 — the end of an era. *(E. Ruddy; APM # 2840)*

And Logging Continues

For most of Algonquin's logging history, the only trees taken were Red and White Pine. Hardwoods were completely ignored — for the very good reason that they don't float, and the water routes were the only way of getting timber out of the Park. This changed with the coming of the railroad, and a significant hardwood industry began to develop in the 1920s, based primarily on the Sugar Maple and Yellow Birch forests of the Park's west side. Hardwood cutting increased greatly in World War II, as many Algonquin Yellow Birch went into plywood used in plane construction, and today Algonquin Park is one of Ontario's most important sources of hardwood for veneer and furniture.

This century has also been one of growing mechanization in the logging industry as a whole. New developments have included the gradual introduction of trucks (beginning in the 1930s) for the hauling of logs, and an expanding network of logging roads throughout the Park Interior. Chainsaws in the 1940s and mechanical skidders in the 1950s, revolutionized the production of sawlogs in the bush. The horses and sleighs of earlier generations of loggers passed into history. There were also sawmill operations in the Park itself, with "small industrial centres" at locations such as Brûlé Lake, Canoe Lake and Lake of Two Rivers.

All of these technological changes created more noise and potential conflict between the loggers and Algonquin's Interior recreationists. As early as 1930, the coming clash was anticipated with the establishment of a 100 foot no-cut reservation around Cache Lake — a lake with many leasehold cottages. By the end of that decade, Superintendent Frank MacDougall had directed the development of a standard system of shoreline, island, and portage reservations from cutting in the face of expanding recreational use, and the recognized need to separate logging and recreation.

One of the first trucks to replace horses in the hauling of log sleighs, in the thirties. A gradual mechanization of the logging industry was underway. (M. McRae; APM # 2401)

A bulldozer replaces the horse in providing the power to raise the barrel to fill this water tanker at J. R. Booth's Maple Leaf camp during the 1930s. *(J. Burchat; APM # 3052)*

The 1940s saw the introduction of the two-man chainsaw — a far more efficient method for sawing trees, especially the hardwoods (which were in such demand on Algonquin's west side). *(Ministry of Natural Resources; APM # 960)*

Mills operated within Algonquin Park, closer to the source of the timber. This McRae Lumber Co. mill (pictured here in 1938) was located on the southwest shore of Lake of Two Rivers, opposite today's campground. Now, little more than a clearing remains. *(H. Taylor; APM # 1283)*

The Omanique Lumber Co. mill on Potter Creek, at the top of Canoe Lake, in 1940. The road in from Highway 60 crossed Potter Creek by way of the wooden bridge in the background. Some mill foundations and part of the bridge remain as visible reminders today. *(J. Leech-Porter; APM # 1270)*

The Coming of the Highway

In the 1920s an Alexander (Sandy) Haggart of Whitney was taking tourists in to Lake Opeongo by horse-drawn wagon along the abandoned railway spur line between the village and Opeongo. At first the trip took a full four hours but by 1929 the railroad bed had been sufficiently improved that it was being referred to as an "automobile road". This was the first way cars could enter Algonquin until the highway was built the following decade.

Highway 60 was constructed through the southern portion of Algonquin Park from 1933 to 1936. The project produced badly needed jobs during these Depression years, and it was to transform Algonquin dramatically in the years to come.

Over 3600 automobiles entered the Park's gates during the highway's first full year of operation, and soon campgrounds had been established at such favoured sites as the Tea Lake Dam and Lake of Two Rivers. At the same time, this new, more convenient means of access to Algonquin made the demise of the railroad just a question of time. Trains did continue to come in from the east as far as the mill on Lake of Two Rivers until 1944, and from the west as far as Cache Lake until 1959 — but on a much reduced basis.

More and more people come to the Park by car. More people meant more Park facilities. During the 1950s, the campgrounds along Highway 60 were expanded. The original Park Museum was opened at Found Lake in 1953 as a centre for the growing program of interpretation of Algonquin's natural and human history for Park visitors. This was followed in 1959 by the Pioneer Logging Exhibit, near the East Gate, later succeeded by the Algonquin Logging Museum nearby, where many examples of the logging tools and equipment shown in this book may be seen first hand.

The highway through Algonquin became famous as a place to feed deer (especially near the Highland Inn where they were fed year round), as a place to see fall colours, and even to hear packs of Timber Wolves.

The portion of Highway 60 lying within the Park was officially designated as the Frank MacDougall Parkway in 1976, in honour of Algonquin's most famous superintendent (1931 to 1941), and Deputy Minister of the then Department of Lands and Forests for the 25 years after that.

It is ironic that, shortly after MacDougall's retirement in 1966, his prediction made 30 years earlier about the increasing conflict between logging and recreation finally came true in a big way. The late 1960s were a time of unprecedented public controversy and debate about the role of logging in Algonquin. Many people had come to feel that logging was incompatible with the wilderness park they wanted Algonquin to be, while the communities surrounding the Park, whose welfare had been tied to Park logging for over a century, saw things quite differently.

Looking westward from the shore of Found Lake in 1935, down the new roadcut for Highway 60, a road construction camp can be seen at the present site of the Education Centre (Old Park Museum) parking lot. Construction of the highway was a government work project during the Depression. (R. E. Green; APM # 2485)

The old West Gate on the south side of Highway 60, at the Park boundary. In 1936, the first full year of highway operation, over 3600 cars entered Algonquin. There were also 6081 Interior users that year — less than one tenth the annual number coming to the Park 60 years later. (H. McRae; APM # 2354)

The new "highway" could be rough in the early days! Here a car is towed to higher ground in 1936. The road was not paved until 1948. (A. Prewitt; APM # 2395)

The first cars entered Algonquin Park in the late 1920s on what had been the railway spur line between Whitney and Lake Opeongo. This is a lunch scene near the lake in those early days. *(Ministry of Natural Resources; APM # 95)*

The original Portage Store, Canoe Lake — a great contrast to the large service centre at the site today. Small outfitting and supply stores were established to cater to the growing numbers of Park visitors, after the highway came in. *(E. Saucier; APM # 1936)*

The feeding of deer along Highway 60 in Algonquin Park soon became a major Park attraction and pastime for day visitors. A large deer herd centred on the Cache Lake area, around Park Headquarters and Highland Inn, where they were fed year round. *(R. Darraugh; APM # 1825)*

Car camping at Lake of Two Rivers during the 1940s. Today's heavier use of the Highway 60 corridor in Algonquin Park began with the postwar recreational boom. The numbers of day visitors, highway campers, and Interior canoeists have steadily increased since then. *(R. Humber; APM # 3264)*

Today and Tomorrow

The Algonquin Park Master Plan was released by the Ontario Government in 1974. Next to Algonquin's creation in 1893, this was probably the most important single event in Park history, and therefore deserves at least a short examination.

The plan was prepared by the Ontario Government in an attempt to resolve the many conflicting demands being placed on the Park, and to set out rational guidelines for Algonquin's future use and development in the face of pressures that can only become stronger in the years to come. The Master Plan's official goal for Algonquin is "to provide continuing opportunities for a diversity of low intensity recreational experiences, within the constraint of the contribution of the Park to the economic life of the region". What this means is that logging will be retained, but that it (and recreational use patterns) will be managed in such a way that the "feel" of wilderness is not destroyed by either activity.

To decide precisely how to do this, the Government carried out over 40 studies, received hundreds of briefs from citizens, held public meetings in Toronto, Huntsville and Pembroke, and appointed an advisory committee representing all interested groups (such as local mayors and M.P.P.'s, leaseholders, the Federation of Ontario Naturalists, and the Algonquin Wildlands League — a group that had done much to focus public attention on the Park in the first place). The recommendations from this advisory committee formed the basis for the Master Plan.

The plan undergoes periodic public reviews and modifications but several major features remain unchanged. One is that the Park is divided into zones each with different allowed uses. Logging, for example, is permitted only in the recreation-utilization zone (about three quarters of the Park) although, even there it is done mostly out of the sight and hearing of recreationists through further restrictions that limit potential logging areas to about 57% of the Park's total area. Other zones include wilderness zones, development zones (like Highway 60), nature reserve zones, and historical zones.

A second major feature of the Plan was the cancellation of the existing patchwork of timber licences held by some 20 logging companies, and the creation of a crown agency called the Algonquin Forestry Authority. It now carries out all logging and forest management in the Park in accordance with comprehensive regulations administered by the Ministry of Natural Resources. The Authority sells the wood to the mills which were formerly supplied by the private companies.

The third area where the Plan introduced far-reaching changes was that of recreation in the Park Interior. In an effort to preserve those qualities shown by studies and questionnaires to be most sought after by the vast majority of Interior users, the Plan called for regulations such as banning motor boats from most lakes, limiting the number of canoeists departing from each access point, limiting the size of Interior camping parties to nine individuals, and banning disposable cans and bottles in the Park Interior.

Many of these provisions continue to be refined and modified particularly in response to periodic public reviews of the Master Management Plan. Thus new chapters are always opening in the on-going history of man's close association with Algonquin Park. Time — and now pictures — will reveal that history to the generations that follow.

We hope you enjoyed this pictorial history of Algonquin and invite you to learn more of the Park's rich past by visiting the Algonquin Logging Museum at km 54.5, opened in 1992, and the human history exhibits of the magnificent Visitor Centre at km 43, opened in 1993 to celebrate Algonquin's first 100 years as a Park.

If you have questions about Algonquin's history or photos you are willing to let us copy for the Park Archives, please address your correspondence to:

> Park Superintendent
> Algonquin Provincial Park
> Ministry of Natural Resources
> Box 219
> Whitney, Ontario
> K0J 2M0

About the Photographs

The Friends of Algonquin Park and the Ministry of Natural Resources wish to acknowledge their deep appreciation to the donors of the photographs in this book, and to all others who have contributed originals or allowed us to make copies for the Algonquin Park Archives. The historical photograph collection now numbers over 6000 pictures — and is of inestimable value to all those who share our mutual interest in Algonquin.

The original sources of the 85 photographs appearing in this book are cited with each picture. The donors are as follows (in alphabetical order): Ottelyn Addison, Archives of Ontario, Rev. William N. Bender, Jack Burchat, Canadian National Railways, Ralph Carswell, Mary (Colson) Clare, Mary S. Cooper, Daphne Crombie, Jean Cunningham (Charles Macnamara Collection), Richard Darraugh, Randolph E. Green, Irma Hambleton, Ralph Humber, Harry M. King, Jack Allan H. Leech-Porter, Dr. Duncan A. MacLulich, Dr. George March (George B. Hayes Collection), Walter S. McNeice (John W. McNeice Collection), Helen McRae, Marjorie McRae, William A. Mudge, Loren Newman, Ontario Ministry of Natural Resources, Mary (McCormick) Pigeon, Ann Prewitt, Public Archives of Canada, Prof. Harry U. Ross (John Walter Le Breton Ross Collection), Edward Ruddy, Essie Saucier, Patricia Swann (Steve Waters Collection), Henry Taylor, Robert J. Taylor, Rose Thomas, Tom Thomson Memorial Gallery, University of Toronto Archives, and Jack Wilkinson.

Permission to reproduce the photographs in this book must be obtained from the donors, through the Algonquin Visitor Centre.